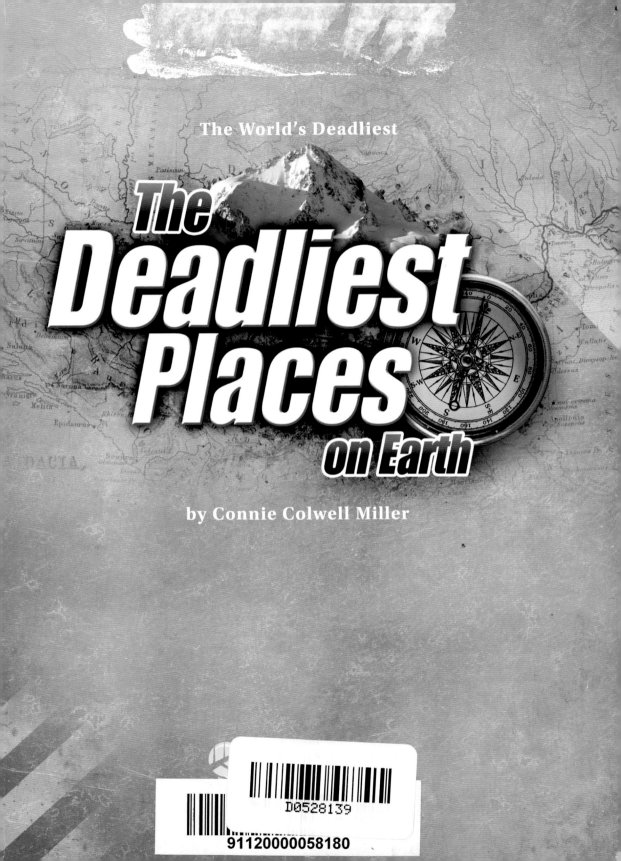

The World's Deadliest

The Deadliest Places
on Earth

by Connie Colwell Miller

www.raintreepublishers.co.uk
Visit our website to find out more information about Raintree books.

To order:
☎ Phone 0845 6044371
🖷 Fax +44 (0) 1865 312263
🖳 Email myorders@raintreepublishers.co.uk

Customers from outside the UK please telephone +44 1865 312262

Raintree is an imprint of Capstone Global Library Limited, a company incorporated in England and Wales having its registered office at 7 Pilgrim Street, London, EC4V 6LB – Registered company number: 6695582

Text © Capstone Press 2010
First published in hardback in the United Kingdom by Capstone Global Library in 2011
Paperback edition first published in the United Kingdom by Capstone Global Library in 2012
The moral rights of the proprietor have been asserted.

Edited by Abby Czeskleba

British Library Cataloguing in Publication Data
Miller, Connie Colwell,
The deadliest places on Earth. -- (The world's deadliest)
910.2-dc22
A full catalogue record for this book is available from the British Library.

Acknowledgements
We would like to thank the following for permission to reproduce photographs: Alamy pp. **15** (Henry Westheim Photography), **19** (© Terje Lillehaug); Corbis p. **5** (Ralph A. Clevenger); Getty Images pp. **7** (Stone/Arnulf Husmo), **8** (Aurora/ Abner Kingman), **25** (National Geographic/ Gordon Wiltsie); istockphoto p. **21** (© jolanta Dabrowska); Photodisc p. **11**; Rex Features p. **29**; Shutterstock pp. **1** (Irina Tischenko), **1** (my-summit), **12** (arteretum), **13** (Michael Klenetsky), **16** (Daniel Gilbey), **23** (tororo reaction), **26** (Heather Lewis).

Cover photograph of a hiker in the desert reproduced with permission of Shutterstock (Galyna Andrushko), (Irina Tischenko), and (my-summit).

CONTENTS

Some words are printed in bold, **like this**. You can find out what they mean on page 30. You can also look in the box at the bottom of the page where they first appear.

DEADLY PLACES

Danger can be found all over the planet. Under the sea. On top of a mountain. In the middle of a desert. The deadliest place of all might surprise you.

SLIGHTLY DANGEROUS

DANGER Meter

DISAPPEARING ACT

The Bermuda Triangle is a strange area in the Atlantic Ocean. Hundreds of ships and planes have disappeared there. No one knows what happens to them or to the people inside them.

DEADLY FACT

Disappearances in the Bermuda Triangle have been blamed on poor weather and pilot error.

ROUGH SEAS

Thousands of creatures live in the sea. But the sea can be a deadly place for people. Huge waves can pull people overboard. Rough waters can sink ships.

DEADLY FACT

Shark attacks are rare but can be deadly.

RING OF FIRE

Most of the world's deadly **volcanoes** are found around the Pacific Ocean. This area is called the Pacific Ring of Fire. It is more than 40,000 kilometres (25,000 miles) long.

DEADLY FACT

More than 400 volcanoes are in the Pacific Ring of Fire.

volcano mountain with a hole in the top that hot liquid comes out of

DEADLY SWAMP

Snapping crocodiles and alligators lie in the **swamps** of the Florida Everglades, in the United States. Deadly pythons slither through the swamp. One wrong step here and you could become dinner.

swamp wet, grassy land

VERY DANGEROUS

FALLING BUILDINGS

Taiwan is a large island off China. Taiwan has more than 200 earthquakes each year. These earthquakes cause buildings to collapse.

DEADLY FACT

In 1999 an earthquake killed more than 2,300 people in Taiwan.

WATER PLEASE

The Sahara is the largest hot desert in the world. The sand is scorching. People who try to cross the desert may die of **dehydration**.

DEADLY *FACT*

The Sahara holds the hottest temperature on record. In 1922, this desert reached over 57 degrees Celsius.

dehydration become ill through not having enough water to drink

DIRTY AND DEADLY

A **slum** is an area in a city that is dirty and overcrowded. There are slums in Bihar, India. People live in overcrowded huts. They have no clean water or electricity. There are no toilets. Many people get sick and die.

DEADLY FACT

Many children in the Bihar slums have to work. They look for things in rubbish tips that they can sell.

slum dirty and overcrowded area in a city

DEADLY JUNGLE

The Amazon rainforest in South America is home to deadly mosquitoes. These insects spread **malaria**. Malaria can cause fever, chills, and death.

malaria serious disease that people get from mosquito bites

DEADLY FACT

Malaria kills more than 1 million people each year.

EXTREMELY DANGEROUS

ANIMAL ATTACKS

The Great Barrier Reef near Australia is home to beautiful sea life. But some sea animals are deadly. The box jellyfish and the blue-ringed octopus are **poisonous**. Their poison can kill a person in minutes.

DANGER Meter

poisonous makes a poison that can cause illness or death

FREEZING TO DEATH

Antarctica is the coldest and windiest place on Earth. Temperatures are as low as -70 degrees Celsius. Antarctica is so cold that people do not live there. Visitors to Antarctica risk **frostbite**.

frostbite when cold temperatures freeze the skin

DEADLY FACT

Antarctica's cold temperatures can kill a person in less than one hour.

TOP THAT

Annapurna in the Himalayas is a dangerous mountain. People climb this mountain for sport. But harsh weather and falls from the rocky cliffs often kill many climbers.

DEADLY FACT

Many people have tried to climb Annapurna. Nearly 40 per cent have died while trying.

CRASH!

You don't have to travel far to find the deadliest place of all. It is your car! Millions of people are injured and killed each year in traffic accidents. Whether climbing a mountain or climbing into a car, be careful. Dangerous places are everywhere.

GLOSSARY

dehydration become ill through not having enough water to drink

frostbite when cold temperatures freeze the skin

malaria serious disease that people get from mosquito bites

poisonous makes a poison that can cause illness or death

slum dirty and overcrowded area in a city

swamp wet, grassy land

volcano mountain with a hole in the top that hot liquid comes out of